Sherlock Puzzle Book (Volume 2)

Bloody Murders of Moriarty Documented by Dr. John Watson

Mildred T. Walker

Table of Contents

Bluesource And Friends

This book is brought to you by Bluesource And Friends, a happy book publishing company.

Our motto is **"Happiness Within Pages."**

We promise to deliver amazing value to readers with our books.

We also appreciate honest book reviews from our readers.

Connect with us on our Facebook page www.facebook.com/bluesourceandfriends and stay tuned to our latest book promotions and free giveaways.

Don't forget to claim your FREE book
https://tinyurl.com/karenbrainteasers

Also check out our best seller book
https://tinyurl.com/lateralthinkingpuzzles

Introduction

I have dedicated my time recounting the events I have experienced with Holmes. These events are, to a varying degree, both gruesome and astounding. Time after time, I am astounded at Holmes' abilities to solve cases. Unfortunately, those moments are also tainted with gruesome deaths and disappearances. Many of those moments have been caused by the infamous Professor Moriarty.

Moriarty did not always work alone. Sometimes, we would come across his work that had been assisted by Colonel Moran. No matter if he worked alone or with help, he was a very sadistic man. Holmes believed him to be the mastermind behind all of the criminal activity in London. Indeed, later on, it was discovered that he, in fact, had many criminals under his control.

Holmes spent much of his time trying to bring Moriarty to justice. This meant that we spent much of our time at crime scenes created at the hands of Moriarty or one of his many companions.

While I have never had the pleasure of meeting Moriarty face-to-face, Holmes has, on occasion, met the man behind the murders. I have no interest in meeting him. I deduce the information about him through what Holmes presents to me. That is enough to stave my curiosity.

Alas, the wealth of information that I have on the murders by Moriarty has provided me with another book. It is unfortunate that I must present you these murder cases for you to solve. I hope that the information herein will be of use to anybody who is unfortunate enough to face a man much like Moriarty. All I ask is that the knowledge found within is used for good.

Dr. John Watson

Answers To The Case of the Confusing Instructions (In Volume 1)

I have to admit that I was confused as well.

"Holmes, could you please enlighten us as to how you figured out the location of Shelley's money?"

"Certainly, Watson, all the numbers that are located in the note represent letters in the alphabet. For example, the first number is 21. The 21st letter of the alphabet is the letter 'U.' If you continue on, you will find that Shelley's money is safe "under the master bed.""

Murder On The Rocks

It was early in the morning when someone banged on our door. I hurried to answer it before they disturbed Mrs. Hudson. On the other side of the door was a large officer from Scotland Yard.

"Mr. Holmes' and your presence is requested at a murder scene," the officers stated.

"This early?" I asked.

"It happened a few hours ago, but we have not been successful in figuring out who killed the man."

Holmes had shuffled his way to the door by this point. He had his pipe in hand and was just about to light a match when the officer said,

"We believe Moriarty may be involved."

Holmes retrieved our coats, handing me mine, before easing out the door past the officer. The walk down the street was silent. The sound of birds was the only thing that entertained our walk. The officer stopped in front of a pub and motioned for us to enter.

Inside the pub sat two men. One man was slumped over the table. The other man sat across from him with a look of shock on his face. Two glasses of clear liquid sat on the table between them.

"How long has he been here?" I asked, referring to the man in shock.

"Since we arrived, six hours ago."

"Have you spoken with him?"

"We have, but it hasn't helped us in the least."

"May I?"

The officer nodded his head. I stepped over to the shocked young man as Holmes investigated the glasses. I could smell the gin as I approached the man.

"Excuse me, but do you think you could answer a few questions for me?"

The man didn't answer, only nodded his head.

"Thank you. Could you tell me what happened tonight?"

"Charles and I were meeting to discuss things of a political matter. We were celebrating, so we both ordered gin on the rocks. I was quite thirsty, so I drank my first down quickly before ordering a second. I drank the second down but waited to drink my third. Charles had only taken a couple of sips from his first after I finished my third. I was about to take a sip from my third when Charles fell over dead."

Holmes picked up a glass and sniffed its contents.

"Both had ice in them?" Holmes asked.

"Yes."

How did Charles die but his friend didn't?

Can You Stop the Killer?

Holmes and I were scouring some case files to deduce the killer of our latest case. We had spent the last week studying the case files, yet we didn't seem to be getting any closer to solving it. I had taken a break to fix us some tea when a knock came from the door.

I stepped to the door and opened it. A small boy stood outside shivering in the cold November air. In his hand, he held a small white enveloped. He reached up to give me the enveloped.

"Who is this from?" I asked.

"I don't know, sir. Some man handed it to me along with this address."

"I see. Did you get a good look at him?"

"No, sir. He was covered in heavy coats and a hat."

"Thank you. Here, for your troubles," I said, handing the boy a three pence.

The boy ran back up the street as I closed the door. I stepped back into the sitting room where Holmes was pouring the tea. I turned the envelope in my hand, studying it. There were no discerning marks, and the only thing written on the front was H & W. Holmes turned and saw the envelope.

"What do you have there?" he asked.

"It's a letter."

"What does it say?"

"I haven't opened it yet. I was checking to make sure that it was safe. It appears to be."

I ran my finger along the seal and ripped open the white paper. I pulled out a piece of paper written in beautiful script. A quick scan of the page told me it had to do with a murder. Whether the murder had happened or would happen was unknown.

"What does it say?"

"My name is Moran, and I have a murderous tale for you. On Friday, a murder took place at 4:21 AM. The morning was a calm morning with light rain. The body of Benjamin was discovered in the dining room. However, it was determined that he had been murdered in the kitchen. When the police arrived, they were unable to discover the cause of death. After an autopsy was performed, they ruled his death as natural. Benjamin, however, was poisoned by arsenic, an undetectable poison. His wife had been called away to take care of her mother late the night before and did not return until 6 AM. She is certain that it was suicide or the butler killed him. The butler leaves home at 4 AM every morning and returns at 6 PM. The butler believes that the wife is the killer because she discovered pictures of her husband with another woman. Who is the killer of the husband?"

Holmes face crinkled into a frown. Something wasn't right with this letter. What it was, I didn't know, but Holmes was certain of one thing. The murder had yet to happen.

Who is the murderer?

Dead In The Park

The trek to the murder was a laborious one and one that I had not intended to make on a windy and snowy Saturday morning. Alas, someone had decided life wasn't interesting enough, and the only way to improve it was with murder.

The beautiful park in the center of London was turned into the gruesome murder scene of a woman named Anne. A young man had taken a stroll through the park earlier this morning and came across her body. She had been shot several times for a reason that is still unknown.

Holmes stepped over to an officer as I knelt next to the body to study her wounds. From my place, I could hear Holmes' conversation.

"Do you have any leads?" Holmes asked.

"We believe we have the suspects narrowed down to six men."

"What are their names?"

"Moran, Charles, Benjamin, Jacob, Moriarty, and Harry."

Holmes glanced over to me as checked the bullet holes. Something caught his eye, and he stepped closer before kneeling across from me. With careful precision, Holmes moved the woman's arm revealing what looked like random letters written in the dirt.

"I think she was trying to tell us her killer," Holmes stated.

"How do those letters tell you that?" I asked.

"It's a cipher, just in case her murderer caught her, she wanted to make sure they couldn't tell what she was doing."

"Well, what are the letters?"

"n q u m f x a g."

Of the six men, who was the killer?

A Dead Party

The festivities of May first were winding down as Holmes and I walked down Baker Street. Our flat was only a few meters away when a young man ran up. He had clearly been drinking, but almost everybody on the street had been drinking.

"You're Sherlock Holmes, right?" the drunk man stumbled.

"Yes."

"We need your help."

The man pointed across the street to a small house that was packed with people. I had noticed the house when I had awoken this morning. They had been celebrating since six this morning. People tumbled around the house and the surrounding streets.

"It's late, just send everybody home," Holmes said.

"It's an emergency. Four people have been murdered."

The man stumbled back across the street to the house packed full of people. Holmes looked at me. I gave him a small shrug. We followed the man over to the house. People had begun to create a small huddle behind the house.

"This was Charles' party. That's him," the man said, pointing to one of the deceased who didn't have any discernible injuries.

I stepped closer to the victims. I could tell right off how the other three deceased had been murdered. One of the men had been beaten with a spade. The second man had been stabbed to death by an uncut diamond. The third man had been clubbed to death. Charles, the fourth man, looked perfectly fine.

"Do you know how long they have been here?" I asked.

"They disappeared a few hours ago. I just discovered them."

"There is something familiar about these deaths," Holmes muttered.

Holmes paced around the bodies. There was something odd about the murders. The question that I wanted to be answered, though, was how the fourth man had died.

How did the fourth man die?

A Sunday Murder

The summer sun beat down overhead as Holmes and I made our way up the winding drive to a large white house. Scotland Yard had requested our assistance in another murder case. It was a rather hot Sunday, and Holmes had been pulled from a game of chess he had been playing with his brother. This made for a bad combination.

The deceased man had been an affluent member of society, so there was no hesitation when it came to calling in Holmes for the investigation. Being in the position he was, there were quite a few people that probably wanted him dead.

As we stepped into the house, we were ushered upstairs to his study. The cause of the death was clear. He had been shot from behind. He likely never knew what happened.

"Are there any suspects to speak with?" Holmes asked, breaking the silence.

"Yes, sir," a young Scotland Yard officer stated, "We have the wife, the cook, and the butler. They were the only three people at home at the time of the murder."

Another office led the three suspects in the room. I continued to study the body and the surrounds to find any clues while Holmes spoke with the suspects. Holmes tapped my shoulder and motioned for me to come with him.

"I don't think you will find anything on the body," Holmes said.

"How do you know? There's always evidence on or around the body."

"All the evidence we need is in their statements."

"How so?"

"Ask them each what they were doing at nine this morning."

I stepped over to the wife who was visibly upset. Her eyes remained focused on the wall above my head, never looking over at her deceased husband.

"Ma'am, can you tell me what were you doing at the time of your husband's death?"

"I was still in bed, sleeping. I had been out late last night taking care of my mother."

"Thank you."

I stepped over to the cook who too had her eyes fixed on the wall. In fact, all three of the suspects were staring at the wall over my head. It was understandable. Most people don't like looking at dead bodies.

"Miss, could you tell me what were you doing at the time of the murder?"

"Yes, sir, I was in the kitchen fixing dinner for everybody. We were expecting company for an early dinner."

"Thank you."

I turned to the butler.

"Could you tell me what were you doing at the time of the murder, sir?"

"Yes, I was outside retrieving the mail."

I turned back to Holmes, a slight knowing grin on his face. The answers seemed harmless enough, but there was one that stood out.

Who killed the man and why?

Frozen On Ice

"The richest man in town was killed late last night in a shocking murder," Holmes began as he read the headline article in the *Daily Courant*, "Commissioner Archer informed us that Scotland Yard with the assistance of Detective Sherlock Holmes and Dr. John Watson are carefully investigating everything and everyone, but they have no lead suspect."

Holmes sighed and looked out the window at paperboy passing out the latest edition. A large crowd of people had begun to gather around the boy to get a paper.

"You would think that there is something better in town to do than read about murder," I said.

"Not for these people. They haven't had a murder in London for a while now. People are longing for something exciting to happen. Other means of entertainment are no longer entertaining to them," Holmes replied.

"It's still a shame that people have such a blood-lust."

"Let's go back over the facts of what we know."

"Mr. Hastings' body was found in the icebox after the mail carrier, Benjamin, contacted Scotland Yard earlier this week to report his suspicion that something was wrong. Normally, receiving a frozen body would be helpful because it preserves the body and the evidence. Unfortunately, there is no evidence to be found. It appears that he was hit in the head with a blunt object, but other than that, there is nothing else to go on. The house has been checked for clues, but there was nothing out of place. Whoever perpetrated this killing was careful. We've talked to all of the people who seem to have had any contact with him, his son Charles, his daughter Anne, and Benjamin the mail carrier."

"There's something we're missing. It's going to be a long night Watson, but I feel we need to go over everything again. I would like to speak with the suspects again."

Holmes and I eased out of the flat, making sure not to draw the attention of the mob down the street. We made our way to the home of George Hastings to speak with his son and daughter once more. Charles Hastings answered the door with a sigh when he saw who it was. He motioned for us to come in.

"My father has more money than anybody else in this town. Anybody would have had a reason to kill him. Surely you can't believe that I did it," Charles shouted, "We got along just fine. When I had dinner with him last month, he told me how proud he was of me for starting my own business like he had."

"Didn't you ask your father for a huge loan to start that business?" Holmes asked.

"Yes, but that doesn't mean I haven't struggled."

"Did you visit your father often?" I asked.

"I would come over every couple of weeks, around once a month. Maybe a couple of times a year. I would have seen him more often, but he had secluded himself inside this house and refused to leave. I had to make an effort to come to see him. I'm a busy man, so it took a lot to make the time to visit."

"I can't believe he's gone," Anne cried, breaking through her brother's diatribe.

Since we had arrived, she had done nothing but cry. It was quite understandable as she had lost her father. The unusual thing was that she only seemed to cry when we asked her a question.

"He was so important to me," she cried again.

"When was the last time you saw your father, miss?" Holmes asked.

"Well, I hadn't seen him in a while, but I talked to him on the phone last Saturday."

"He didn't mention being worried about his life?" I asked.

"No, he sounded fine. I'm sure you are insinuating that I had a motive to kill my father since I will inherit a lot of money, but Charles will inherit just as much. Charles even owed father a lot of money, the money he borrowed to start his business."

"We're not insinuating anything, Ms. We are trying to make sure we have all the information. Since you and your brother were the only people who had regular contact with him, we thought you could provide us with more information. I can see you have shared all that you know. Thank you for your time," I said.

Holmes and I left as Anne and her brother began to argue over who had a better motive. As we walked back down the street, we met the mail carrier.

"Excuse me, do you have a moment to speak?" I asked.

"I do. What do you need?"

"Can you tell us what you knew about Mr. Hastings?" asked Holmes.

"Nothing much. I was used to his mail piling up because he didn't like to leave his house. I would have a package for him every now and then. He would always be eager to receive the packages, so whenever I had one, he would answer the door. I know it doesn't seem like much, but when he didn't answer his door the other morning, I knew something had to be wrong."

"Did you notice any other suspicious activity lately?"

"No, sir, not that I can think of."

Holmes and I walked back home. I could tell something was working in his mind. He didn't say much, and every now and then he would sigh. Suddenly, he stopped and turned to me.

"Our victim was reclusive and hardly ever made contact with anybody. There are no clues, plenty of motives, and no witnesses. I can only think of one person who gains from all of this."

"What do you mean?"

"What person in the city of London gains from a murder?"

Who does Holmes suspect the murderer is?

Murder At Moriarty Mansion

Monday hadn't gone the way Holmes and I had planned. Early that morning, a letter had been slid under the flat door. Holmes had quickly opened the letter. Inside was an invitation to a party at a local mansion. The mansion, at one time, had been home to Moriarty. Ever since he began his crime spree, he no longer used the house, and a member of the Tuck family had taken up residence there. Holmes had long believed, though, that the new owner was still working for Moriarty.

The events that transpired that night may well have increased Holmes' suspicion. Many people of the upper class were in attendance. Five guests that caught my and Holmes' attention were Mr. Tuck, Ms. Peck, Sir Marlow, Lord Kent, and Ms. Grigg.

The night started out innocent. So innocent, in fact, that I had begun to believe it was just an ordinary party. But I was wrong. Mr. Perry was found dead in the office of Mr. Tuck. As soon as he was discovered, Holmes and I began speaking with the guests to try and figure out who could have killed him. The trouble was our main suspects, Tuck, Peck, Marlow, Kent, and Grigg, had all, at some point, went into the office at different times, with different weapons, motives, and clues that incriminated them.

First, Holmes and I spoke with Mr. Tuck.

"I didn't do it. I didn't leave a footprint because one of the women did. I went into the room before the person who took in the poison. I must say though, she was there for a quarter of an hour before somebody else went in."

Then we spoke with Ms. Peck.

"I do admit I took in the revolver, even though my motive wasn't for revenge. A man went into the room after I was in there and his motive was either blackmail or rage."

Next was Sir Marlow.

"All I know is I did leave behind a fingerprint, but that doesn't explain why Ms. Grigg lost a hair, does it? The person who was in there 70 minutes before I took in a lead pipe."

Then we met with Lord Kent.

"I went in after a woman who didn't take a rope in because the last person who had gone in did. I was in there for more than 35 minutes confronting Mr. Perry with my motive, which, I must say, wasn't blackmail or greed."

Lastly, we spoke with Ms. Grigg.

"Yes, I was in the office. My motivation was jealousy, but it wasn't as bad as that man's blackmail motive that went in at five minutes past nine. I went into the office before another man who left behind the clue of a drop of blood."

Holmes and I stepped to the side after the interrogations were finished. I had written all of the information in my journal and was no more aware of the killer than I had been before the interviews.

"The murderer entered the room at half past ten," Holmes stated.

"How do you know?"

Who is the murderer?

A Killer Dinner Party

Two nights ago Holmes and I were called out to the scene of a murder. Mr. Exeter had been murdered by one of his guests at his dinner party. An officer greeted us and told us that he had already taken everyone's statement and let them go.

"You let the guests go," Holmes shouted.

"Yes, sir, they had already been questioned, and I didn't see the use in them staring at the dead body."

"You don't let anybody go until I get to speak with them."

"I wrote down everything they said."

"Did you speak with your superior before letting them go?" I asked.

"No, sir, I thought it was the appropriate thing to do."

"Please leave us your notes and go have a word with your superior. I'm certain he will have something to say about your choices this evening."

The officer handed Holmes his journal and disappeared into the house. Holmes handed me the journal and wandered over to where the body laid slumped over the table.

"Read me the notes as I look around," Holmes stated.

"The suspects are Margaret, James, Oliver, Noah, and Jane. The murder took place in either the sitting room, observatory, dining room, conservatory, or bedroom. The possible weapons are a rope, poison, knife, gun, or candlestick."

"Is there any more information, or is that all he provided us with?"

"There is actually a few more notes."

"Continue."

"Either Noah was in the dining room, or the man with the knife was in the sitting room. Either James had the rope, or Noah was in the observatory. Either Oliver was in the conservatory, or James was in the bedroom. The five suspects are Jane, the person in the bedroom, the person in the dining room, the person with the rope, and the person with the knife. The woman with the poison was not in the dining room. The rope was in the sitting room, and the gun was in the bedroom."

Holmes paced around the room before coming to stand beside me. He glanced over the journal in my hand.

"The body was found in the observatory, so we know where he was murdered," Holmes stated.

"Yes, now the only thing we have to find out is who did it and with what."

Who is the murderer, and what weapon did they use?

Mid-Afternoon Murder

Holmes and I sat at the fireplace and watched as the snow fell outside. We had been enjoying a holiday treat that Mrs. Hudson had prepared for us when a knock came from the door. I slipped to the door, pulling my robe around me as the cold air blew in.

"I am sorry to bother you this afternoon, sir, but your presence, along with Mr. Holmes, is requested at the site of a murder," a young Scotland Yard officer said.

I didn't recognize the officer. He must have been a new officer. Holmes had walked up behind me.

"Who are you?" Holmes asked.

"I'm Alfred. I just began working with Scotland Yard. This is my first case."

"I see. I suppose we should get dressed. Where is the murder?"

"The estate of Mr. Charles Barnum."

"We will meet you there."

"Yes, sir."

Holmes and I dressed and left out in the cold afternoon to the scene of the murder of Mr. Charles Barnum. He was one of the wealthier men in London and was famous for having never married. When we arrived, the officers had pulled together the people who had been in the house at the time of his murder; the cook, the maid, two friends, and his niece. Both the maid and the cook lived in his house, and the other three guests had slept over the night before.

The five suspects had all been lined up in front of a large bow window. Given the position of the window, and the time of day, Holmes and I had a perfect view of the setting sun.

Alfred, the officer who had come to our flat, stepped up to us with the details that he had uncovered thus far. All of the suspects had agreed that Charles Barnum had been discovered murdered in the morning, shortly before 6:30 AM, but he had still been alive a few minutes after midnight when they had all gone to bed. Nobody had heard anything during the night. Emily Barnum, his niece, had come downstairs to the kitchen to get a glass of water, and as she walked back upstairs, she had passed the bow window where she noticed her uncle's dead body.

Holmes nodded at the officer for his information. He stepped to the suspects and began to interrogate the suspects. The provided the following information:

The maid replied with, "I retired to my room shortly past eleven after I had finished cleaning the dining room where Mr. Barnum dined with his guests. I then helped the cook put away the leftover food. I read a book until around 12:20 and heard the occasional laughter and talk, although I couldn't understand what was being said. This morning, I was awoken by a scream, which had come from Ms. Emily, so I rushed down with the cook and his two friends. Mr. Barnum was lying dead in front of the window. The office moved his body just before the two of you arrived. I didn't hear anything happen, but whoever did it could have muffled the shot some way. I'm innocent, though."

The cook told us, "It's like the maid said. She was cleaning the dining room while I cleaned up the kitchen, and we both stored the leftovers and talked for a few minutes about Mr. Barnum's guests. I went upstairs to my room around the same time she did but fell asleep after I had finished dressing for bed. That would have been about 11:30, and I slept soundly until the scream this morning woke me up. I rushed downstairs with all of the others, and there was the body. I tell you, it wasn't me. I've been with Mr. Barnum for eight years, and he knew he could trust me."

Next, Emily said, "I was up until midnight with my uncle and his friends, talking and joking. I fell asleep at around 1:15, but I woke up at 6:24 and I was thirsty. I went downstairs to the kitchen to get a glass of water. On the way back upstairs, as I passed by the bow window, the one here, I could see a beautiful sunrise outside, but, sadly, my uncle was sprawled on the ground with blood all around him and shot through the head. I screamed, and the others were here within a couple of minutes."

Before the first of the two friends could speak, Holmes held up his hand to stop him from saying anything.

"That's enough. I know who murdered Mr. Barnum."

"We haven't spoken with the others," I said.

"Trust me."

Who killed Charles Barnum, and how did Holmes know?

A Suicidal Murder

Holmes and I had been called to a murder at a local Inn. The Inn was located about three kilometers from the victim's home. As we stepped into the room, I saw the body of the man lying peacefully in the bed. The day was January 7th, 3:15 PM. The maid of the Inn had been the unfortunate soul to discover the body. The man was Sean O'Shay. He was in his late 20s, owned a successful business, taught Sunday school, and had a loving wife and child. Holmes shook his head and turned to me.

"Why do you think somebody like him would commit suicide? It doesn't seem like something he would do," Holmes asked.

"It does all seem a bit odd to me, too," I replied.

Holmes and I were treating this as a murder. While everything pointed to a suicide, there was a chance that somebody he trusted had killed him. According to what his employees had to say, along with close friends and family, there were only three people he trusted: his sister, Martha, who he was very close with and who assisted him in his teachings at the local church; his brother, John, who owned his own business; and his wife, Jenna.

It looked as if he had been poisoned. While poison wasn't nearly as messy as a gunshot wound or a beating, it probably wasn't the fastest way to die. Depending on the dose and the type, the poison could have taken a few seconds to a few minutes to kill him.

Holmes searched through the room as I continued to study the body and the bed that it lay on. A piece of paper was slid onto my journal, causing me to look up. Holmes had found what appeared to be a suicide note.

4, January 4:10 AM

To my dear loved ones,

Jenna, Sis, John, I would just like to tell you how sorry I am. Blame God for why I am to die today. Blame Him. Seek Him if you want to know why I did leave you. Do not mourn my death. Please move on.

Goodbye,

Sean

"Why would his last words be so abrupt and impersonal? Why would a Sunday school teacher blame God?" I asked.

"Those are my questions as well."

The coroner had arrived and packed up the body. Holmes and I had spent the next few days talking to people who had known him the most. Then we received word from the coroner. He had found that the poison would have killed him instantly, but he hadn't been dead more than three hours before his body was discovered.

"That means the date and time on his note were false," Holmes stated.

We asked the three people mentioned in the note if the handwriting looked like Sean's. They had all agreed that he had written the note.

"The note," Holmes said.

"What about the note?"

"He gave us a clue to who killed him in the note."

Who is the killer?

Murder On The Railway

One night Holmes and I were awoken by a banging on the door. Before I could get to the door, I heard Mrs. Hudson answer the door with a shout.

"Why are you here at this ungodly hour?" she yelled.

I eased up beside Mrs. Hudson, tapping her shoulder gently.

"I can handle this," I said.

"You better. I don't want people at my flat at this time of night."

Mrs. Hudson trotted back to her flat. I turned my attention back to the gentleman at the door. He looked rather frightened. I wasn't sure if it was due to Mrs. Hudson or whatever business he had come here with.

"I'm sorry it is so late, but it's an emergency," the man stated.

"Why didn't you contact the police?"

"I was told to come to 221b Baker Street and speak with Sherlock Holmes and John Watson."

"I see, come in then."

I stepped aside and let the man step in. Holmes was in the sitting room when we entered. He was already dressed for the day. Either he hadn't dressed for bed, or he thought it was already morning. Either way, he was ready for what was about to transpire.

"I work for the railway," the man stated, "The express train just contacted me. A murder has happened. They requested your immediate help."

"Is there anything you can tell us about what happened?" I asked.

"The only thing they were able to rely on is that only a handful of passengers were still on the train. As it struck midnight, the lights went out, and when they were relit, the passengers were alarmed to find that one of the passengers was dead. That's when they contacted me. They asked for Mr. Holmes by name."

With that information, Holmes and I left with the young man to meet with the train. Holmes was great at interrogations. Over his time as a detective, he had learned, though, that witnesses were often mistaken or would contradict their own statements. In a situation like this, he would often only ask them a single question. He would ask them to tell him one thing that they could clearly and absolutely remember from what happened when the crime took place.

As soon as we arrived at the train car that held all of the passengers, Holmes began to look over the train. There were only ten passengers aboard. He went from passenger to passenger asking them to tell him one thing that they were certain happened during the moment's right before the lights went out in the train cars. What the passengers said is as follows,

Mr. S said, "I was dining with Mr. J."

Mr. G said, "There was the same number of men and women in my car."

Mr. J said, "Mr. K was not in the dining car."

Ms. L said, "Mr. Q had just entered my car."

Mr. F said, "Ms. W and Ms. P were talking to one another in hushed tones."

Mr. R said, "Mr. G was not in the passenger car."

Mr. Q said, "There were fewer women in my car than the other."

Ms. P said, "Ms. L was not in the same car as me."

Mr. K said, "Ms. P was in the passenger car."

Ms. W said, "Mr. F was avoiding Mr. R and hiding behind a newspaper in the opposite car."

The conductor sat off to the side, watching as Holmes completed his interviews and I scribbled notes in my journal. Holmes turned around and announced that he knew who had killed the passenger.

"But it's impossible for you to figured out who the murderer is simply from a bunch of seating arrangements," the train conductor exclaimed, "You don't even know which car the victim was seated in."

"To the contrary, my good man," Holmes answered, "It is the curse of a killer that he has to answer any question regarding the murder that he has committed with a lie. The innocent person only tells the truth, but the lone murderer has betrayed themselves by their testimony."

Who is the killer?

An Office Murder

Holmes and I entered the office of Mr. Butler. His faithful secretary, Mary, stood outside in a mass of nerves. An officer had retrieved us from our residence an hour earlier. As we walked through the house, the same officer met up with us to share with us the information he had learned from Mary.

1. Mr. Butler has been murdered. The murderer stabbed him with a sharp, thin knife through the back of his chair and right through his heart.

2. The house had been wrecked, but there was nothing missing. Some of the sheets of paper that laid on his desk had coffee stains on them, but Mr. Butler did not drink coffee. In the office, there were no coffee containers. There were a couple of gloves on the floor.

3. Mary had written down only three announcements in her visit book: Joseph Edwards (2:35), Louis Williams (3:10), and Mark Grey (3:45). Mary said that Mark was the only person to serve himself a cup of coffee.

4. They found the disposed cup of coffee in Mary's wastebasket. Mary claimed that Mark entered Mr. Butler's office with the cup in his hands, and then he left it sitting on her desk, so she took it and disposed of it.

5. There was no evidence on the knife, but Mark's fingerprints covered the cup the coffee had been in.

6. Mr. Butler's watch was broken, presumably due to a fight, and it showed the time was 3:50.

Holmes didn't say a word to the officer. He turned and walked outside to where Mary stood. Turning to the officer that stood next to her, he said,

"Take her into custody. She is the killer."

Why did Holmes suspect Mary as the killer?

A Deadly Dance

Holmes and I had been invited to a New Year celebration at Lord Charles' mansion. This was a regular party that took place every year. For the last few years, Holmes and I had avoided the party. The first time we had attended, Moriarty had tried to kill Holmes. Holmes had agreed this year because he suspected that something was going to happen.

Lord Charles and his wife Abigail strolled through their party, shaking hands and greeting people. A large brass band was conducted by Herbert Edward. The evening was filled with elegance and opulence that most of the guests enjoyed. I didn't feel any of it. It all felt very heavy like something was waiting to happen. As the clock struck twelve, my heavy feeling turned real. The lights in the ballroom went out, submerging us all in darkness. I felt Holmes at my side.

"Stay here, don't move," he said.

I did as Holmes had said. We stayed standing next to each other as the other guests stumbled around trying to find their way in the darkness. Eventually, somebody lit some candles, allowing us to see. As people began to regain the boundaries, somebody screamed. Holmes and I ran towards the scream to find Lord Charles laying in a pool of blood.

"Somebody contact Scotland Yard," Holmes said, "As we wait, I'm going to do some preliminary investigation."

"Why are you investigating things?" a woman asked.

"I am Sherlock Holmes, and this is Dr. John Watson. We have worked on a number of murder cases with Scotland Yard."

Holmes and I made our way through the party guests, speaking to each one until we had a list of five suspects: Benjamin, Tom, Edward, Herbert, and George.

"I have followed through on all necessary leads to find out who murdered Lord Charles," Holmes stated, "and I conclude that it's a mystery."

Before anybody could say anything, Holmes took hold of the killer's arm.

Who murdered Lord Charles?

A Murder At The Circus

Whenever the circus came to London, things would always get interesting. I still hadn't figured out the interest in watching people with peculiarities parade around with deadly animals. Alas, it was a lucrative pastime for those involved. This morning, though, the show had been canceled as Holmes and I made our way to the scene of the murder at "Uncle Walt's Traveling Circus."

John and James Jenkins had been found dead. They were locked inside of Willy's Dancing Bear cage. Both boys had been mauled by the bears and were covered in bite and claw marks, leaving them torn to shreds. Upon reaching the crime scene, Holmes took note of two offices accosting Mr. Willy rather savagely.

"You need to confess to the murders. We know you did it. The boys were found in your bear cage," the officer said.

"No, it wasn't me. The kids did bother me a lot, but I would never lock them in with the bear," the man said.

Holmes and I calmly walked over to the men.

"What's going on?" Holmes asked.

"This man, he's the killer. He locked the boys in there so that the bear would kill them. There are others who heard him threatening the boys on several occasions since the circus came into town."

"But, sir, they had been threatening me as well. I never once said that I would lock them in with the bear. I wouldn't wish that kind of death on anybody."

"Hold on, let me make sure that I have the whole story before I hear any more accusations," Holmes stated.

The officer calmed himself down enough to explain what the situation looked like. It seemed that John and James belonged to a small animal rights group in London. This group, as small as it was, had been organizing protests against the circus months before it ever arrived in town. They were upset about the pony rides, the trick dogs, but they were really upset about the dancing grizzly bear.

Willy had raised the bear from a cub and had been trained to perform tricks and dance. Willy insisted that the bear was well-cared for and he loved to perform. Still, the protestors continued to protest.

John and James had moved past harassing Willy and had started to threaten him if he didn't allow the bear to go. Willy had tried to explain that the bear wouldn't last long in the wilderness since he had been hand-raised, but they didn't believe them. Several of the circus workers had witnessed these confrontations, although none was certain if Willy had threatened to harm them in any way. However, it was said that the boys were determined to free the bear by any means possible.

Holmes thought for a moment over what he had just been told.

"What evidence, aside from the threats, have you found that leads you to believe that Willy locked the kids in the cage deliberately?"

"We believe the boys died sometime around midnight last night. The whole circus was celebrating the bearded lady's 30th birthday last night, and Willy was seen leaving at 10 last night."

"I told the officers that I didn't feel well. I had a bad reaction to the shrimp that they had served. I went home to sleep."

"And you didn't hear anything once you arrived here?" I asked.

"No, my trailer is at the front of the lot. All the animals are kept in the back, plus, I had taken some heavy medication to help me sleep. With my age, I can hardly hear anymore."

"Stop making excuses and tell them about the key," the officer said.

"What key?" Holmes asked.

"The key to the bear cage. Seems that Willy had to get a new one for the brand-new lock on it and he doesn't have a copy of it."

"Is that true?"

Willy nodded sadly, "It is. The bear almost chewed the old one off. I had to replace it yesterday."

"What happened with the old key?"

"I threw it away. There was no reason to keep it."

"Did you see anybody else on the grounds?"

"No, there is no way for a person to get in the front. The back, possibly, but you would have to have a ladder in order to cross the fence."

"Officers, please take him to his trailer and wait outside for me. Watson and I are going to take a look at the crime scene."

The officers left with Willy while Holmes and I checked out the bear cage. The bear had already been removed, but the bodies of John and James were still inside.

The boys were barely recognizable due to the damage that the bear had inflicted. I am not ashamed to say that this was one of the horrendous murders I had ever seen. Both boys laid near the still locked cage door. Near them were a bent and stained key with a pair of wire cutters. Holmes looked to the roof of the 20-foot cage. The sides were made up of metal bars, but the top of the cage was covered in metal mesh. Some of the mesh had been bent around the middle. On the outside of the cage, a large ladder lay against the back.

After a quick study of the murder scene, I followed Holmes as he walked back to the officers.

"I believe that you owe Willy an apology," Holmes said.

"Why?" the officer questioned.

"What we have here is a sad and ironic accident, but there has been no murder. And if we speak with John and James' activist friends, they will confirm my suspicions."

What clues did Holmes find? What really happened to John and James?

A Murder Of Five

Holmes and I had been called away to a murder one autumn day. The murder, or as we soon found out, murders took place at what we called the Moriarty mansion. As we stepped inside, we were greeted by an officer who pointed us over to the Commissioner.

"Thank you for arriving so quickly," the Commissioner said.

"What do we know?" Holmes asked

"Well, this is a special case. We already know who the killer is."

"Then why are we here."

"The killer asked for you two."

"Where is he?"

"That's the second thing. We don't have him in custody. We don't even know where he is. He left us a letter. It seems that he wants us to play a game."

The Commissioner handed the letter over to Holmes who quickly read over it. He then handed the letter to me. This is what it said.

Hello, Holmes. I am certain that Dr. Watson is with you as well. Today, you will find five people have been murdered, each in a different room with a different weapon. The way the bodies will be discovered is not the way in which they were killed. Below you will find six clues, which I am certain you will be able to use to solve the mystery of these five people's murder. For the sake of my hand, I shall refer to the victims by initials only.

1. The murder with the lead pipe was not done in the hall or the library.

2. Mr. G was not murdered in the kitchen.

3. The rope was not the murder weapon used in the library.

4. Neither Mrs. W nor Ms. S was murdered with the candlestick, the revolver, or the lead pipe.

5. The person who was murdered in the billiards room had just finished having dinner with Ms. S, Mr. G, the person done in the with the candlestick, and the victim of the rope.

6. Neither Mr. G nor Mr. P was killed with the lead pipe, in the hall, or in the library.

Best of luck,

Moriarty

I folded the letter and placed it in my journal and looked over to Holmes. His face was blank.

"We have to solve it."

What room were the victims killed in and what weapon was used?

A Killer Laundry

Holmes and I arrived at the scene of another murder in the early afternoon. Our lunch had been interrupted, but I believe that Holmes prefers to work on the case rather than eat. I took notes as we surveyed the area. Of course, I know that Holmes wouldn't need the notes. He and I both took note of the smashed window that led to the laundry area. The small and well-maintained gardens out front looked amazing in the midday sun. I couldn't help but think what Mrs. Hudson would think of their roses.

Holmes and I made our way to the door where a plump lady claiming to be the owner's sister greeted us.

"Hello," Holmes said calmly, "I am Sherlock Holmes, and this is Dr. John Watson. We are here to inspect the scene."

The plump lady stepped to the side and let us in. The first thing I noticed was to the left. It was the dejected figure of a sobbing man sitting on the couch. Holmes and I stepped over to the man.

"Could we ask you a few questions?" I asked.

"Yes… I will do my best," he said between sobs.

"Can you tell us what happened?"

"I was in the laundry with my brother as we were planning out what clothing we need to have washed for the coming week. I heard something that sounded like a gunshot come from outside. I ducked at the sound. My brother feels dead. I ran out of the room, slammed the door, which likely startled the killer. I tried to see who was out in front, but all I hear was running. The gate slammed shut and whoever killed him was gone."

"I see, and didn't you see anything of the killer? Clothing maybe, hair color, shoes?"

"No, that's all I saw."

"Thank you. We may need to ask you a few more questions, but we are good for now."

Holmes and I made our way over to the laundry, where the murder had taken place. Holmes grasped the doorknob and pushed the door open. The body of the victim was against the door, so he had to push fairly hard to get it open. After the door was pushed far enough for us to enter, Holmes scoured the room, again checking the smashed window, this time from the inside. I knelt next to the body and checked the gunshot wound and the body.

"I've seen enough," Holmes said, marching out of the laundry room.

I took off after him and returned to the man that was crying on the couch.

"I'm afraid that your tears do not fool me. You will have to come with Dr. Watson and me to Scotland Yard."

Why does Holmes believe that the brother killed his own brother?

A Murdered Wife

It had already been a long day when Holmes and I were called out to a murder scene. They wouldn't have called had it not been for the fact that Moriarty had left behind his calling card, yet he insisted that he hadn't actually killed the woman. The only thing we knew for certain was Moriarty had something to do with it.

After we made our way inside the house, I knelt over the body and began my initial assessment of her wounds. The woman was lying on the sofa having been beaten.

"It appears that she has been hit in the back of the head with the butt of a pistol three or four times," I stated.

The pistol was still on the floor next to the body. One of the officers was studying the pistols for evidence but didn't appear to be having any luck. Holmes studied the rest of the room.

"Have you contacted her husband?" Holmes asked.

"Yes," the officer said, "He was contacted at his office, and I asked him to come home. I haven't given him the bad news. I hate having to break this kind of news to people."

"I'll do it," Holmes offered.

The coroner had arrived and was removing the body from the scene. Holmes took a seat in a chair as we waited for the victim's husband to arrive. As the coroner left, the husband arrived. Making his way into the sitting room, he said,

"Where's my wife? What has happened?"

"I'm sorry, sir, but your wife was murdered about three hours ago," Holmes said, "Your maid found the body and contacted the police."

"I am unable to find any evidence on this gun," the officer stated, "I'll have to send this to a specialist."

The husband's face flushed with anger as he said, "Please locate the fiend that clubbed my wife to death. I will supply the person who catches him with a substantial reward."

"Save your money," Holmes said, "The murderer won't be that hard to find."

Who is the killer?

The Periodic Murder

Holmes and I were called to University College to help investigate the murder of one of its top chemists. When we arrived at the scene, the body hadn't been touched. Since I am a doctor, they allowed me to examine the body. The chemist had been brutally stabbed numerous times. From the trajectory of the knife wounds, I determined there had to be two people who killed the chemist.

"Excuse me, officers, have you found any murder weapons?"

"Not at this time."

"Thank you. You need to be looking for two knives that are about 23 centimeters long and two and a half centimeters wide. One assailant is left-handed, and the other is right. From what I am seeing right now, there are at least 22 stab wounds. That means that each man stabbed him 11 times each."

Sherlock walked up about that time. "How do you know it was men, Watson?"

"The chemist stood around two meters. The angle of the stab wounds indicates the suspects were of an equal or slightly taller height. I've not seen a woman of that stature during my lifetime as of yet, Holmes."

"Very good, Watson now what can you make of this?"

Sherlock handed me a piece of paper with some numbers written on them: 42 – 75 – 18 – 22 / 42 – 88 – 7.

"What am I supposed to do with these numbers, Holmes?"

"I was hoping you would tell me what they meant."

"Right now, I'm not so sure. Let me think about it while I'm looking around."

"By all means, Watson help yourself."

I began walking around the room looking at different things when a periodic table of elements caught my eye. I grabbed a piece of paper and pen and quickly jotted down some notes.

"Holmes, come quickly. I know who killed the chemist."

What had Watson found?

The Murderous Scheme

Holmes and I were called to Charing Cross Hospital where a woman had been brought in with a gunshot wound to the head. She was barely hanging onto life and was unable to tell us who had shot her.

The officer standing outside her room didn't know any specifics but said they were still at her house investigating. So we decided to go and see what we could find. On the cab ride, there Holmes was in a very solemn mood. Murder cases were always rough to work, especially when it was a female victim.

The cab pulled up outside, we climbed out, paid the fare, and walked around the outside of the house. There weren't any visible footprints outside the house, and we couldn't find anything out of order inside the house. We ruled out it being a robbery gone wrong since not a single thing was missing inside.

The cleaning girl was sitting on the stairs with her head in her hands. The officers had told us her name was Katherine. I touched her shoulder, and she jumped out of her skin.

"I'm sorry, Katherine I didn't mean to scare you. Can you tell me what you saw when you came to work today?"

"Oh, God, it was awful. I used my key to let myself in. I went to the kitchen to get breakfast started and made ma'am a cup of tea. I was taking the tea service up to her. I opened her door, and all I saw was the blood."

Katherine broke down into hysterics again.

"Is she married?"

"Yes."

"Was he here when you arrived this morning?"

49

She frowned. "Um, no I don't think so. I haven't seen him at all, coming to think about it."

"Does he work at home?"

"No, he works in town. He's a teacher at the local school."

"Have you noticed anything missing?"

"No. I've not really looked around. The officers told me to sit here and not move. I really need to use the facilities."

"You go do what you need to do. Just hurry and come back to me."

"Okay, thank you."

Katherine went off down the hall and was back in a few minutes.

"Katherine, do you feel like looking around to make sure nothing is missing?"

"Sure, where would you like to start?"

"Anywhere you want to."

She led us from room to room without finding anything at all out of place or missing.

"Thank you, Katherine. You can go home now. Where can we find you if we have any more questions?"

I wrote her address down in case we needed it, but I really didn't think we would. It all seemed to me to point to somebody who lived here. We just needed to find her husband to tell him of the shooting. We decided to go back to the hospital to see how the lady was doing. By the time we arrived, the doctors informed us that she had died.

All of a sudden, the doors were slung open and a man came running into the hospital. He was stopped by a doctor and an officer.

"Sir, can I help you?" asked the doctor.

"Who shot my wife? I stopped by the house, and Katherine said my wife had been taken to the hospital."

"Sir, where were you last evening?"

"What does that have to do with my wife being shot?"

"Just answer the question."

"Fine, I was at my good friend Professor Moriarty's house playing poker last night. It lasted a lot longer than I anticipated and decided to just stay the night instead of trying to find a cab to bring me home in the dark."

Holmes stepped forward. "Officer, arrest this man."

Why did Holmes want him arrested?

The Apple Murder

Holmes and I were walking through the countryside when we saw a crowd forming outside a house. Wondering what was going on, we went toward the crowd to figure out what was happening.

"Holmes, want to make a guess as to what is happening?"

"No, dear Watson, I would rather wait and figure it out for myself."

We walked along in silence trying to catch any bits of information as we could. We saw a woman sobbing on the porch talking with the constable. Holmes, recognizing the constable, walked up to him.

"Hello George, what has happened?"

"Holmes, did we call for you?"

"No, we were just out on a walk and happened on the scene." Holmes pointed my way. I raised my hand to the constable.

"You might as well go inside and see what you can make of it. Nobody else has any ideas."

"Could you inform me of what has happened up until now?"

"This is Mrs. Dorothy Smithers. She found her husband died a few hours ago."

Holmes tipped his hat to her. "I'm sorry for your loss."

Mrs. Smithers nodded her head and sniffled, "Thank you."

"Do you feel like telling me what happened?"

"I'll try." She took a few deep breaths. "I went out this morning to see a sick friend. My husband was lunching with his friend Professor Moriarty…"

I could see Holmes clench his teeth at the mention of Moriarty's name.

"...I left them food on the stove to eat. I told them I would be home by four o'clock and to enjoy themselves. When I left, they were playing a game of chess. I got home around four and found him on the floor."

"Was Moriarty still here?"

"No. I didn't poison the food, I promise."

"I'm sure you didn't, Mrs. Smithers. Do you mind if my friend and I have a look around your house?"

"I don't care. Go ahead."

Holmes and I went into the house. Mr. Smithers was lying on the kitchen floor. There was a pool of vomit beside the body. We were careful not to disturb anything. We found a knife and remnants of an apple on the table.

Holmes was crawling around on the floor looking for any speck of evidence. He gets obsessed when he is trying to prove Moriarty was guilty of a crime. We had to figure out how Moriarty killed Mr. Smithers. There were remnants of two halves of an apple and the kitchen knife. I was completely stumped when Holmes jumped up and said,

"I know how Moriarty did it."

What did Sherlock figure out?

The Snow Murder

Holmes and I were called to Scotland Yard to help investigate a murder. A body had been found in a snow-covered field. Their top investigators were stumped. There was a set of footprints in between two parallel lines with a third line cutting between the footprints. The police didn't even have a clue as to what or who to look for. They were beginning to think that the guy committed suicide, but nobody can shoot themselves in the back of the head.

Who does the police need to be looking for?

Richard's Murder

Holmes and I were called to the house of Richard Westall. He was a very wealthy man who lived on the north end of town. His house was huge, and he employed many people. Scotland Yard was convinced that whoever killed Richard was the same man that killed Miss Delilah a month ago.

"Watson, I know this was done by Moriarty. He's taunting me again. He has to always be one step in front of me. One of these days, he is going to slip up, and I will catch him."

"I have no doubt you will find him and bring him to justice, Holmes. Just don't lose sight of what's in front of us. We don't even know where he was killed or which weapon killed him."

There wasn't much to go on. All we do know is that Richard was found outside in the garden, but Holmes was convinced he was placed there after he was murdered. There weren't any bloody drag marks so whoever killed him either carried him outside or cleaned the blood off the floor.

The constable handed Holmes a list of suspects and as he figured Moriarty was on the list. The other suspects were a young man who lived in town Frank Brown, and an elderly woman who lived next door, Mrs. Grey.

Holmes began walking through the house looking for any clues Scotland Yard might have missed. When he, unfortunately, couldn't find anything, he asked for all the suspects to be brought into the formal sitting room. The weapons that could have been used were lying on the table. There was a gun, a kitchen knife, and a long piece of rope. He looked around to see Moriarty standing there smiling smugly.

"Moriarty."

"Holmes."

Everyone looked at each other as you could cut the tension with a knife.

"I will prove that you did it, Moriarty."

"You will try, my good man."

"Watson, are you ready with your notebook?"

"Yes, Holmes ready and waiting."

After we had talked to all the suspects, we had a list of things we needed to sort out. The only thing we knew for certain was that the murderer had access to a gun.

1. The person who had the knife was in the kitchen.

2. Mrs. Grey didn't like the chaise lounges in the lounge, so she stayed clear of the room.

3. Moriarty was complaining to the cook for most of the evening.

4. Whoever was in the bedroom was on the opposite side of the house where the gun was located.

5. Moriarty didn't have access to the rope even though the staff said he had a knife in his room to protect himself against an assassination attempt.

Who murdered Richard? What weapon was used? What room did they do it in?

The Gaslighting Murder

Holmes and I were out walking when a hysterical man passed us heading to Scotland Yard. Being the curious chaps we are, we followed to find out what had happened.

"I need some help. I just returned home and found my entire family dead in their beds."

The officer sitting at the closest desk stood up.

"Was there any blood present?"

"I didn't look for blood. I just opened their doors and called their names. Nobody moved. I knew they were dead."

Holmes caught the officer's eye.

"I might be of some service if it is okay with Scotland Yard?"

The man turned around. "Who are you?"

Holmes extended his hand to shake this man's hand.

"Allow me to introduce myself, my name is Sherlock Holmes, and this is my associate Dr. John Watson."

The man shook Holmes' hand. "Nice to meet you, my name is William Dutton. Are you an officer?"

"No, sir but I do work with Scotland Yard on some cases when they need me to. I would be glad to help you out if you want me to."

"If it's okay with Scotland Yard, it is okay with me."

Holmes looked at the officer. The officer nodded his head.

"We are short-handed due to that cold that has been infecting everyone in town. It would be great Mr. Holmes if you could take the lead on this. Send for us if you need anything. If you leave me your address, I'll send the coroner to your house."

We waited for the man to give the officer his address and headed out. It wasn't a long walk, and we tried to talk with the man as we walked. He wasn't very talkative, so we let the conversation lull. We arrived at his house, and he slowly walked up the three steps to his front door. He could tell he didn't want to go back into the house.

"Mr. Dutton, would you like to sit out here while we take a look around?"

"Would that be okay?"

"Sure, when the coroner gets here to send him up, please."

"Yes, sir."

Holmes and I walked into the house. We didn't see anything out of the ordinary. There was no overturned furniture, no broken windows, or anything out of place. We proceeded through the house.

The first bedroom we found had two beds in it. There was a child lying on their side in each bed. I looked at Holmes. He was just standing there staring at the bodies. I took a deep breath and proceeded into the room. I gently turned the children over and checked for a pulse. I didn't find a pulse on either child. I bowed my head, said a little prayer, and covered their faces.

I walked past Sherlock and headed toward the next room down the hall. I opened the door, and the exact same scene was in front of me. Two beds, two children both lying on their sides covered up to their necks, neither had a pulse. I again bowed my head, said a prayer, and covered their faces.

Holmes continued to stand outside the rooms not moving and not saying a word. I walked to the stairs and paused with my hand on the railing. I turned toward Holmes who still hadn't moved.

"Holmes, are you coming upstairs with me?"

He slowly turned his head toward me, but his eyes were unseeing.

"No, Watson, you go on ahead."

I proceeded up the stairs and found the master bedroom. I slowly opened the door. What lay before me sent chills down my spine. Mrs. Dutton was lying on her side with a baby clutched to her chest. I didn't want to touch either one but knew I had to. To my horror, both mom and baby were dead. Again, I bowed my head, said a prayer, and covered their faces.

I turned around to see the coroner standing there.

"How many in this bed?"

"Two."

"That makes a total of six. What in the world happened here, Dr. Watson?"

"I don't know yet, but Holmes and I will get to the bottom of this. I promise you that."

"Who in the world would want to kill a mother and her children?"

"I might have the answer to that."

We both jumped because we hadn't heard Holmes walk up behind us.

"Holmes, you scared the life out of me. What have you figured out?"

"I'm on to something, but I need to go talk to Mr. Dutton."

What had Sherlock figured out?

The Beach Murder

Holmes and I were taking a holiday at Babbacombe Beach. We were walking along the rocky edge of the sand looking for driftwood and shells. Holmes had found some pretty pieces of driftwood that will look nice on the mantle. Some could even be used as presents for Mrs. Hudson and some of the other tenants.

The winds started howling, and before we knew it, a storm was upon us. There was thunder, lightning, and heavy rain. We had to shield our faces to keep the sand that was whipping around from cutting us. We got as close to the face of the cliff as we dared. We found a shallow cave that was just deep enough to give us some shelter.

"Hopefully, this storm will blow over quickly, Holmes."

"I hope so. If not, we are either going to have to tough it out in here tonight or brave the weather and walk until we find shelter elsewhere."

"If we are in here after the sun goes down, it is going to get very cold. We might have to burn our driftwood to keep us warm."

"Nonsense, Watson there is plenty of driftwood out there that is worthy of being burned. We won't have to burn the pretty ones."

"I hope so, Holmes."

There was an especially bright flash of lightning. It was soon followed by a big crash of thunder. It made both Holmes and I to jump out of our skins.

"Good news, Watson. The storm is almost over."

"How can you know that, Holmes?"

"Simple, when the lightning flashes, just count until you hear the thunder. This will tell you how close the storm is to you. After that last one, I counted to 23 before the thunder rolled. Trust me, the storm is dying down."

"Thank goodness."

It wasn't long before the winds died down and we were able to leave the shelter. We were making our way up the road from the beach toward the city. A man comes running up to us screaming that his wife has been killed. He grabbed Holmes by the arm.

"Please help me, my wife has been killed."

"Sir, I'm not a police officer, but I will help you find one."

We walked along until I spotted an officer walking along the street. I flagged him over.

"Yes, good sirs, what can I help you with?"

Our new companion grabbed at the officer. "Please, you have to help me. My wife has been killed."

"Where?"

"Back at the beach."

"We were at the beach. We didn't see anything out of the ordinary."

"It was on the north side of the beach."

Holmes began rubbing his chin. I knew that look in his face. He was thinking about something. The officer began asking the stranger more questions.

"What else happened that you can tell me?"

"Well the storm came out of nowhere, and we were walking along the top of the cliff. We were almost on the path when I heard a huge clap of thunder. It startled me, and I turned around to see where my wife was. I heard my wife scream when a large flash of lightning happened. I ran to the edge of the cliff and saw my wife lying at the bottom of the cliff mangled among the rocks. I saw the shadow of a man running away from me on top of the cliff."

"Officer, this man is obviously lying. Arrest him."

What was the man lying about?

The Exter Murder

Holmes and I were asked by Scotland Yard to help solve the murder at Exter Manor. Holmes was in rare form today. He had been on a cocaine binge and hadn't slept in for two days. He swears he is perfectly fine to work a case so off we go.

We climbed into the hansom cab Scotland Yard sent for us and settled back to endure the 30-minute ride to the Exter Estate. Sir Exter was a widower who only employed three people. It was said that he had left his entire estate to one of his employees. There was Yvonne, the cook, Allyn, the butler, and Edward, the gardener. When we arrived at the manor, all the employees were waiting in Sir Exter's office. Holmes walked in puffing on his pipe looking very much like the calm, cool, and collected detective he was.

"Hello, everyone, my name is Sherlock Holmes. This is my associate, Dr. John Watson. Could you please introduce yourselves to me and tell me a little bit about yourself?"

Each employee stepped forward one at a time. The first one to step up was Yvonne, the cook.

"Hello, Mr. Holmes and Dr. Watson, my name is Yvonne, and I am…was Sir Exter's cook."

"Hello, Mr. Holmes and Dr. Watson, my name is Allyn. I am the butler."

"Hello, Mr. Holmes and Dr. Watson, my name is Edward, and I am the gardener."

"Thank you, we would like to talk with each of you one at a time. Edward would you please stay? We will start with you. Everyone else, please go into the sitting room. We will call for you when we are ready for you."

"Sure, Mr. Holmes."

The other employees filed out and down the hall. I stood at the door to make sure the others went into the sitting room. Once I knew we were alone, Holmes began interrogating Edward.

"Edward, what can you tell me about your coworkers?"

"What do you mean?"

"Have you ever seen any of them try to harm Sir Exter?"

"No, but I have seen Allyn trying to steal Sir Exter's ruby."

"Anything else?"

"No."

"Very well, could you please send in Yvonne?"

"Yes, sir."

Edward headed off down the hall and within a few minutes, Yvonne timidly knocked on the door. I opened the door to find her standing there meekly picking at her fingers.

"Hello, Yvonne. Have you ever seen Edward or Allen trying to hurt Sir Exter?"

"No, but Edward is always sneaking around. He makes me feel creepy."

"Anything else?"

"No, not that I can think of."

"Very well, could you please send me Allen?"

"Yes, sir." She did an excellent curtsy and left the office.

She headed off down the hall, and Allen was at the door.

"Hello, Allen. Have you even seen Edward or Yvonne try to hurt Sir Exter?"

"I don't know if it is relevant, but a few times when I was in the kitchen, I would see Yvonne sprinkling something in Sir Exter's food. She always said it was just spices, so I didn't question her further since I know nothing about cooking."

"Thank you, you can go back to the sitting room. We will go over our notes and get back with you as soon as possible."

Who could have killed Sir Exter?

The Double Train Murder

Holmes and I were called to Scotland Yard to help investigate a double murder on a train. The train station managers were getting irritated because they weren't allowed to let any trains leave until we got this murder solved.

The driver of the train was in the engine compartment while the conductor was at the caboose. The officer on board thought they had been shot at the same time since he had heard the shots go off at the same time.

Holmes boarded the train and walked the entire length of it. He stopped in the very center of the train.

"Watson, how fast was the train traveling?"

"According to my notes, the train was traveling at 150 kilometers per hour."

"Those men were not killed at the same time."

How did Holmes know this?

The Suicide Scheme

John Hawkins decided to go home for lunch from the office. When he entered his flat, he saw his wife hanging from the ceiling. He ran out into the street screaming for help. It just so happened that Holmes and I were walking by in just that moment.

Holmes stops the man. "Sir, what is the matter?"

"My wife hung herself."

Without hesitating, we go running into the man's flat. Sure enough, there she hung. I couldn't stand seeing her swinging back and forth, but I knew I couldn't cut her down until Scotland Yard got there.

"Sir, I need you to go get Scotland Yard. We are going to look around while you are gone if that is okay?"

"Sure, yeah, I can do that."

I stood under her to keep her body from swinging. Holmes moved the chair that was lying underneath her feet, and we immediately knew the women hadn't committed suicide.

How did we know it wasn't suicide?

The Candy Murders

It was a lazy Sunday afternoon. I was reading the newspaper while Holmes played his violin. Nothing of interest was catching my eye until one story with the headline "Candy Murder." Now I knew I had to read it. The article read like this:

Detectives of Scotland Yard are investigating another murder involving candy. Each victim has been poisoned by candy that contained cyanide. The latest victim was 50 years old named Joe. On the table beside the victim were nine other candies. These didn't contain cyanide. This murder is very suspicious since Joe's two-year sentence had been overturned.

The detectives have been investigating other murders that were very similar, and none of these have been solved. A 30-year-old man named Jeff had his ten-year sentence overturned just two weeks ago. The very next day, he was murdered the exact same way as Joe. The only difference was there were only three pieces of candy left on the table.

Another man named John who was 46 had his four-year sentence overturned about one week ago had been found with five candies near his body the next day after he was released. Jim, aged 35, had his five-year sentence overturned a couple days ago to be found dead just yesterday with six candies.

Detectives are perplexed about these cases. Anyone who can help should come forward.

I quickly read the article to Holmes.

"Let me get this straight. Did every person eat candy before they died?"

"That's what the article said."

"Everybody who died was a criminal who had their sentence overturned?"

"Yes."

"Moriarty did it, but he had help this time."

Who helped Moriarty kill all these men?

The Church Murder

"Holmes, have you seen the paper this morning?"

"No, I've not read it yet. Why? Is there something interesting in it?"

"Yes, Abigail Dunner was shot in the church cemetery yesterday."

"Interesting. What else does it say?"

"Well, the police say the shot was fired from the bell tower that stood about 23 meters high. It is located on the opposite side of the church from the cemetery."

"Do they have any suspects?"

"Yes, Reverend Paisley." Holmes raised his eyebrows at the mention of the reverend's name.

"It says that he didn't like the way she would show off and make everybody else feel bad about themselves during church functions. The next suspect is Abigail's niece, Margaret. She says her aunt made her feel inferior because she wasn't as wealthy as her. The last suspect is Lord Westerly. He didn't like the way Abigail always made fun of his disability."

Holmes had been sitting quietly with his fingers steepled.

"Elementary, dear Watson."

Who killed Abigail?

The Baker's Murder

I was in the mood for a pie, and I knew I wanted to try the new bakery in town. Wilhelm had just moved into town from Germany. He had lived in England for two years working in a bakery there to save money so he could open his own shop. He also wanted to bring his wife here from Germany. He was a very nice man but barely spoke enough English to get by. It helped that I knew some German from my time in the Army.

"Holmes, I am in the mood for some pie. Would you like to walk with me to Wilhelm's bakery?"

Holmes stretched. "Yes, I think a walk about town would do me some good. Otherwise, I will just sit here and sleep."

We donned our coats and hats and proceeded out the door. The day was sunny but not too hot, and my spirits were immediately lifted. I took deep breaths of fresh air.

"I feel better already, Holmes. It's amazing what fresh air can do for the body."

"I do feel more awake. I was going to hail a cab, but now, I think I want to walk. Are you up for a little walk, Watson?"

"I am if you are."

"Then, let's go."

We walked in relative silence enjoying the day and each other's company. That was what was so good about having decent companions. Sometimes words don't have to be spoken to enjoy each other.

We rounded the corner where Wilhelm's bakery was and ran into a crowd of people who were gathered in front of his shop.

"Excuse me, what has happened?"

"Someone said that Wilhelm has killed himself."

"Holmes, Wilhelm would not have killed himself. He loved his bakery and was getting ready to send for his wife. Something isn't right."

"I agree." Holmes started making his way through the crowd.

The front door of the bakery was still locked, but you could see Wilhelm lying on the floor with blood pooled under his head. He had a small gun clutched in his right hand. This sent alarms off in my head. The constable was just opening the door by the time we made it to the front of the crowd.

"Hello, Mr. Holmes, Dr. Watson can you believe this?"

"No, I can't. There have to be more clues inside."

The constable stood to the side, "By all means, go ahead and see what you can find. I'll control the crowd."

There was a suicide note lying on the counter next to a letter addressed to Wilhelm. The note stated that Wilhelm's wife had been killed in an accident back in Germany. His suicide note read, "I had almost reached my goal to be able to reunite with my wife. Now it is going to be sooner than I originally thought. I no longer have a will to live." On the bottom of the note instead of his name was the letter "M."

I turned to Holmes.

"He was murdered."

How did Watson know Wilhelm had been murdered?

Answer: Murder on the Rocks

"Moriarty has some new tricks," Holmes said, swirling the gin in the glass.

"Moriarty?" the shocked man asked.

"The man who killed your friend and most likely wanted to kill you."

Holmes sat the glass back down and leaned over to inspect the man slumped over the table.

"Do you know what happened?" I asked.

"The man was poisoned."

"We both had the same drink."

"Yes, but you drank yours quickly."

"How does that affect poison?" I asked.

"The ice was poisoned. The deceased sipped his drink giving the ice a chance to melt, thus introducing the poison to him. You, on the other hand, downed your first two drinks. You didn't give the ice enough chance to melt."

Answer: Can You Stop the Killer?

"This killing hasn't happened," Holmes stated.

"How can you be certain?"

"There hasn't been a calm Friday morning with rain in months. This is a game. Somebody is toying with us."

"That means we could possibly stop this from happening."

Holmes stopped pacing and stared at me. I could see the wheels in his mind working hard to come to a conclusion.

"But first we have to figure out who the killer is going to be," Holmes said, breaking the silence.

"The only logical killer would be the writer of this letter, Moran. He knows all the details and the wife and butler both have an airtight alibi."

"Watson, you are brilliant. This means that Moriarty is back at work. Moran only works with Moriarty."

Answer: Dead in the Park

The letters didn't mean anything to me, not at that moment, but Holmes' mind was at work. He turned to the officer and asked him to list the possible suspects of the murder. I quickly grabbed my journal and scribbled down the names Moran, Charles, Benjamin, Jacob, Moriarty, and Harry.

"I believe she moved the letters up in the alphabet according to their location in the name," Holmes muttered.

"Do you know what the name is?" I asked.

Holmes didn't respond. Instead, he continued to stare at the letters until he said,

"Moriarty is the killer."

"How do you know?"

"M plus one is N, O plus 2 is Q, R plus three is U, I plus four is M, A plus five is F, R plus six is X, T plus seven is A, and Y plus seven is G."

Answer: A Dead Party

Holmes continued to pace between the bodies and the street. Suddenly, he stopped and knelt next to the bodies.

"Do you see what I see?" Holmes asked, pointing at the bodies.

I looked over the bodies again, taking in everything. I saw the bodies, the obvious killings on three, and the perfectly clean fourth body.

"I'm not sure. What do you see?"

"What else do you know of that has a spade, diamond, and club?"

I thought for a moment before replying,

"A pack of cards."

"What's missing?"

"Hearts… The last man died of a heart attack."

"Moriarty did this."

"How do you know?"

"This has every characteristic of a Moriarty scheme. We need to keep an eye out, and figure out how he caused Charles to have a heart attack."

Answer: A Sunday Murder

The three suspects all had an alibi, but I knew, as did Holmes, that one person was lying. Why the killer had decided to stay and not flee the scene was something I would never understand. The fact that they have such an easily seen through alibi was another conundrum that I would never discover the answer to.

"Well, Dr. Watson. Who do you believe the killer to be?" Holmes asked.

"You mean you believe one of us did it?" the wife asked.

"Yes, ma'am, but rest assured that you are not the killer."

"The killer is the one who is lying. That would be the butler. The mail is not delivered on Sundays. I would have chosen a smarter alibi or left the scene if I were you," I said, addressing the killer.

An arrogant smile spread across his face as he reached into his pocket. A Scotland Yard officer grabbed his arm, assuming the man was hiding a gun.

"It's a letter," the killer said.

Holmes nodded to the officer to let go of his arm. The killer reached into his pocket and pulled out a white envelope and handed it to Holmes. The wife and cook left the room as the officer took the killer into custody. Holmes ripped the envelope open and pulled out a square sheet of paper.

"What does it say?" I asked.

"M."

Answer: Frozen on Ice

Holmes marched down the street towards the building for the *Daily Courant*. I followed quickly behind as he stepped up to the door of the office of James Walsh. Mr. Walsh opened the door and stepped aside to let us in.

"Who gave you information about the murder of Mr. Hastings?" Holmes asked.

"I spoke with you and the Commissioner shortly after it happened. Do you not remember talking to me? The information I received wasn't much," he replied.

"I remember. Have you received any more information?"

"No, the Commissioner told me that you would inform of any new information. Why, do you have something for me?"

"Yes, we have a lead suspect. Do you remember what you said in your article? How the city's richest man was murdered late Saturday night?"

"Of course."

"How late?"

"Well... egads."

"Indeed. The last time a person was in contact with Mr. Hastings, that we are aware of, was Saturday. Due to the nature Mr. Hastings body, and the fact he was accustomed to allowing his mail to pile up, we cannot determine a time of death. The best estimate of the time of his murder is sometime between Saturday and Monday morning when the body was discovered. But somehow you have come up with a more specific time of death. Shortly after I read what you wrote, I know you or your informant knew more than an innocent person could. Now, you have told me that it was you. This story of yours has gone on long enough."

"Fine, it was me. Do you know how frustrating it is to be a journalist working for Moriarty? Nothing has happened in months because he is waiting for the right time. Finally, I had a chance to write about something interesting."

Answer: Murder at Moriarty Mansion

Holmes took my journal and pen and drew out 10 grids of 25 squares. He handed the grid back to me and told me to make off the squares that matched up with information we had been given. Once Holmes had finished going over the information we had, I compiled the grid into a simple list.

Mr. Tuck entered the room at 9:05 with a dagger. His motive was blackmail, and he left behind a note.

Ms. Peck entered the room at 11:25 with a revolver. Her motive was greed, and she left behind a footprint.

Sir Marlow entered the room at 11:55 with a rope. His motive was rage, and he left behind a fingerprint.

Lord Kent entered the room at 10:45 with a lead pipe. His motive was revenge, and he left behind a drop of blood.

Miss, Grigg entered the room at 10:30 with poison. Her motive was jealousy, and she left behind hair.

With the information in front of me, I turned to Holmes who was already walking towards the killer.

"Ms. Grigg is the killer," I said.

"Indeed."

Answer: A Killer Dinner Party

Holmes walked back over to the body as I looked over the notes once more. I began to write down the information I had been given into different rows and columns. I quickly discovered that Margaret had been in the bedroom with the gun. James had been in the sitting room with the rope. Oliver had been in the conservatory with the knife. Noah had been in the dining room with the candlestick. Jane had been in the observatory with poison.

"Holmes," I shouted, motioning him to come back over.

"Do you have something?"

"Jane was the only one that was in the observatory at the time of death. She had the poison as well, which matches the fact that there are no marks on the body."

Answer: Mid-Afternoon Murder

Holmes motioned for me to step around the suspects and up to the bow window. He pointed outside to the setting sun.

"What do you see out there?" Holmes asked.

"Nothing but the sun."

"What's it doing?"

"Setting."

Holmes nodded and turned back to the suspects. He motioned for Emily to step forward. He pointed out the window once again.

"You see the setting sun?" Holmes asked.

"Yes."

"Tell me, is this the same window you said you saw the sunrise from."

"Yes."

"That's impossible, my dear. The sun sets in the West. There is no way you could have seen the sunrise through this window. You are the killer."

Emily's upset face turned hard as she glared at Holmes. She pulled herself away from Holmes and stared out the window.

"I had been promised part of his estate, but we had a bit of dispute over a certain Professor that I often worked for. He was coming downstairs as I was returning to my room, so I took the time to speak with him about our differences. He informed me he had already disowned me and he wasn't going to re-include me in his will. I had found a pistol while I was in the kitchen, so I shot him. Trust me, though, I was doing him a favor. He died a much more peaceful death than he would have at the hands of Moriarty."

Answer: A Suicidal Murder

Holmes had asked the three people mentioned in the note to meet us at Scotland Yard. He had spent the night before scouring the note for information about the killer.

"I asked you three here today because one of you killed Sean O'Shay," Holmes stated.

"But he committed suicide," Jenna exclaimed.

"That's what the killer wanted us to think. I studied the suicide note and found that he had left a message for us. He wrote the time as 4:10 AM, but he wasn't referring to the time. He was referring to Genesis 4:10, which is an excerpt from the story of Cain and Abel. In this excerpt, an envious Cain kills his brother Abel. Many pieces of information in the note led to this conclusion. AM refers to the Old Testament. In his note, Sean, being a Sunday school teacher, also hinted to searching for God to determine who killed him by saying 'Seek Him if you want to know why I did leave you,' which refers to the Bible. Furthermore, he intentionally avoided using his sister's name in the letter. Instead, he wrote, 'Jenna, Sis,' which sounds a lot like Genesis. This all led to the conclusion that John killed his brother."

Answer: Murder on the Railway

Holmes, as any good detective does, starts by assuming that everybody was telling the truth about each other's location. He and I came up with the following seating arrangement of the train cars: S J L Q G R (2 women, 4 men) in the dining car, and K P W F (2 women, 2 men) in the passenger. We understood that both R and F were interchangeable in this scenario, but as both are men, the precise position of both of these men was irrelevant at this point. This seating arrangement contradicted G's statement that there was an equal number of men and women in his car, which was the dining car, as well as the statement of Mr. Q's that there were fewer women in one car than the other.

Thus, Holmes knew that both G and Q had to be telling the truth and someone was lying about their occupancy. Holmes continued that only one possible configuration could make both of these men's testimonies true: G, two other men, and three women in one car and Q, two other men, and one woman in the other.

Because G and Q had to be in different cars, Holmes worked through his witness list to find the lie that had placed Q inside of the wrong car. The first statement of Q was when L said that she and Q shared the same car. If this was the lie, it would leave S J L G R in the dining car and put K P Q W F in the passenger car, but this would keep G and Q's statements inaccurate.

This meant that Ms. L was telling the truth. Next was P's claim that placed L, and by extension, Q in the other car. If P was lying, it would place S J G R in the dining car and K P L Q W F in the passenger car. Again, this didn't match G or Q's statements.

Holmes was now certain that Mr. G, Mr. Q, Ms. L, and Ms. P were telling the truth. He looked at Mr. K's statement, who had established where P was positioned. Assuming that K was the liar, this would place S J P G W R in the dining car and K L Q F in the passenger car.

Holmes being Holmes, he doubled checked his work by running back through each remaining statement against his reasoning. This proved that K was the only possible person whose lie would be able to make every other witness' statement true.

"That is why I believe Mr. K is the killer," Holmes stated.

Answer: An Office Murder

"Holmes, how do you know she killed him?" I asked.

I couldn't help but notice that Mary didn't seem all that surprised by the announcement. Still, I wanted to know why he felt that she had to be the killer.

"First, the watch couldn't have been broken during a fight. It is easy to see that there was no struggle because Mr. Butler was stabbed in the back, so the broken watch was a setup. Secondly, the mess, as well as the coffee, was a setup because we know that there was no fight, and it would be hard for Mark to enter and put on gloves to fight with a cup of coffee in his hands. Lastly, the cup of coffee only had Mark's fingerprints. If Mary had touched the cup, which she said she did, her fingerprints would be on it as well, unless she had gloves on."

Mary stepped closer to Holmes, a smug grin stretched across her face. She pointed a finger at Holmes and said,

"Moriarty says hello."

Answer: A Deadly Dance

"Holmes, what are you doing?" I asked.

"I told you who the killer was."

"No, you said it was a mystery."

"Yes, I said it was a Mr. E. The murderer, as you can see is Mr. Edward."

Answer: A Murder at the Circus

"How do you know?" the officer asked.

"First, the metal roof of the cage was damaged. Secondly, there were wire cutters in the cage. Why would Willy need to cut open the top of his bear's cage to throw in John and James? Didn't he have his own key? If Willy had put the boys in the cage, he would have pushed them through the front door. Then, there is the ladder that was leaned against the back of the cage. Do you have any idea of how that got there, and why it was placed there?"

The officers didn't respond to Holmes' question.

"Simple, Willy had said that you would need a ladder to get in the back over the fence. They wouldn't be able to get in through the front, but they were more interested in freeing the bear, so they needed to go through the back anyway."

"What do you mean?" the officer asked.

"This is my last clue," Holmes stated, holding the key.

"That's my old key. I threw that away," Willy cried.

"You did, which may have been the mistake, but you couldn't have known that the boys would try to do something this foolish."

"Mr. Holmes, are you saying that John and James placed themselves in the bear cage?"

"Yes, I am. They used the ladder to get over the fence in the back and then used it to reach the top of the bear cage. They cut their way through the wire mesh of the cage, and they had planned on using the key to open the front door to set the bear free."

"But that key doesn't work for the new lock," Willy cried.

"Yes, you and I know that, but John and James didn't. They likely found the key near your trailer while visiting the circus and thought they could use it to set chuck free."

"So they locked themselves in with the bear."

"I'm sorry, but yes, they did. Since your bear is a very territorial grizzly bear, he must have woken up by the sounds of John and James trying to desperately open the lock, which is why the key ended up getting bent. He smelled the strangers and attacked them. Nobody was around to hear them cry for help and they foolishly didn't bring along any rope to help them get out of the cage because they thought they would be able to get through the front door."

Holmes and I said goodbye to Willy and followed the officers over to the animal activist friends of John and James. They admitted that they knew that the boys had planned on trying to release the bear, but they had done nothing to stop them.

Answer: A Murder of Five

"We know who killed them, we don't have to play Moriarty's game," I said.

"Yes, we do."

Holmes held his hand out for the letter, and I handed it back to him. He wouldn't listen to reason now. He felt he had to solve the puzzle that Moriarty had given him. I found out later that he believed that Moriarty would find out whether or not he had solved the puzzle. After a few silent moments, Holmes reached for my pen and wrote down the answers.

"Mrs. W was killed in the hall with the rope. Mr. G was killed in the conservatory with the revolver. Mr. P was killed in the kitchen with the candlestick. Mr. M was killed in the billiards room with the lead pipe. Ms. S was killed in the library with the knife."

Answer: A Killer Laundry

"I don't understand," the brother said.

"You were fairly convincing with your tears, but the murder scene revealed your lies," Holmes explained.

"How so?"

"It's very simple, you claimed that you heard the shots, checked on your brother, and found that he was dead, you ran from the laundry room, and slammed the door. The problem with that is that when Dr. Watson and I entered the room, the body was leaned up against the door, which means that nobody had exited the room since he fell against it when he was shot. You wouldn't have been able to get out of the room with the body against the door. Instead, you were the one outside that shot your brother, and you chose to stay at the murder scene."

"It was worth it, though," the man started, "Moriarty promised me great things if I cleared a path for him."

Answer: A Murdered Wife

"What do you mean the murderer won't be hard to find?" the husband asked.

Holmes crossed over to the man standing over the officer and the gun.

"How did you know that your wife was clubbed to death?" Holmes asked.

"I... just assumed."

"Watson."

"Normally, when a gun is involved, people will assume that the person has been shot," I explained.

"I must have been told before I arrived."

"You were not aware of the fact that your wife was dead until you arrived home, sir. I know the officer who contacted you did not tell you anything more than to return home. The only way that you would know that your wife had been beaten would be if you beat her yourself."

Answer: The Periodic Murder

Holmes walked over to where I was standing. He looked at the piece of paper and back at me.

"Are you sure?"

"I checked each number twice. Look for yourself."

Holmes took the piece of paper and compared it to the periodic table of elements.

"The numbers stand for elements. This spells: Mo – Re – Ar – Ti / Mo – Ra – N. Moriarty and Moran."

He looked up at me with the biggest smile on his face.

"We'll get him this time, Watson."

"I hope so."

Answer: The Hospital Murder

The doctor looked shocked when Holmes demanded the man be arrested. In fact, the man himself looked a bit shocked.

"Why are you arresting him?"

"Two reasons, doctor. One, he couldn't have talked to Katherine because we had already sent her home after we talked with her this afternoon. Two, nobody but we, Katherine, and the killer would have known that she had been shot."

"How could have I shot her? I was at a friend's house all evening."

"That might be true sir, but your wife was shot early this morning. You could have easily left Moriarty's house early and gotten home before Katherine arrived, shot your wife, and left again until you knew it was safe to make your little entrance here. There were no signs of forced entry, no robbery, and nothing had been disturbed. I'm sure your good friend Moriarty helped you plan this little scheme. I don't know what your motive was but you, sir, are under arrest."

Answer: The Apple Murder

"Holmes, what have you figured out? How did Moriarty kill Mr. Smithers?"

"What clues do we have Watson?"

"The only clues I know of are remnants of two apple halves and a kitchen knife."

"Exactly, Watson, now what does that tell you?"

"I don't know, Holmes. It looks to me like if Moriarty had placed poison on the knife, they would have both died."

"Yes, that is true. Could he have done anything else?"

"Holmes, you clever man, I would never have thought of that. He placed the cyanide on just one side of the knife and made sure to feed that half of the apple to Mr. Smithers."

"Yes, Watson, I can't wait to stop that man."

Answer: The Snow Murder

Moriarty was planning what he thought was going to be the perfect murder. Mr. Jonathan Tuttle owed Moriarty a substantial amount of money. Mr. Tuttle wasn't a very good poker player and had lost over 1,000 pounds to Moriarty.

Moriarty had sent for Jonathan to come to his house earlier this evening. He was giving him one last chance to pay his debt before taking drastic measures. Jonathan knocked on Moriarty's door at precisely six o'clock. Moriarty opened the door sitting in a wheelchair. His leg was bound in a cast and was sticking straight out.

"My goodness, Jim, what happened?"

"Oh, just a silly little accident, I will be fine in a few weeks. How are you doing?"

"I'm doing fine. Did you need my help since you obviously can't get around that well?"

"The only thing I need from you is the money you owe me."

"Jim, I've told you it's going to take me a couple months to come up with the entire sum. If you would just allow me to pay you a bit along with each paycheck, it would be easier for me."

"Easier for you, yes, let's make your life even easier. I'm stuck in this chair, and you can go anywhere you would like. Does that seem fair to you?"

"No, Jim, it doesn't. Hey, why don't I work my debt off? I could do whatever you need to be done around the house. I can be your legs."

"Jonathan, I like for my debts to be paid in full in cash. I've given you more time than anyone else. I'm done waiting. Why don't we go for a walk?"

"A walk in this weather? It's snowing like crazy."

"I like the cold. What do you say? Are you up for a walk with a man who can't walk?"

"If that's what you want to do sure, let's go for a walk."

"We will have to go out through the garden. It's the only route that is suitable for a wheelchair."

Jonathan started out pushing Moriarty's chair until he had maneuvered it out of the garden and into the snowy field.

"You can stop pushing me now. Why don't you walk in front of me to check for holes and rocks in the field, so my wheelchair doesn't get stuck or knocked over."

"Sure, Jim."

They went far enough out so that the body couldn't be seen from the path. Moriarty drew a gun from underneath the blankets draped over his legs. He took aim and fired. The bullet struck Jonathan in the back of the head. He fell forward, dead. Moriarty rolled the wheelchair in the exact same path as when he went into the field, so there weren't any more marks in the snow. As soon as Moriarty returned home, he took off the fake cast and threw the wheelchair into the fireplace so he wouldn't leave any evidence behind. He went into the garden and swept away the wheelchair marks, so nothing led back to his house. He had done it, the perfect murder or so he thought.

Holmes was never too far behind Moriarty...

The police needed to be looking for a man in a wheelchair.

Answer: Richard's Murder

After a long lengthy discussion, Holmes and I had finally figured out where everyone was and who had killed Richard.

"Watson, we had to have figured something wrong. This can't be right."

"Holmes, we've gone over all the facts and clues a dozen times. This is where all the clues are pointing us. You've always said the clues won't lie and to always listen to the clues. This is correct. You just have to face facts."

"I know, Watson, I was just so sure."

"I know, Holmes. Let's go tell them who gets to leave and who doesn't."

We walked back into the sitting room. All the suspects stood up except Moriarty. He had a little arrogant smile on his face.

"What's wrong, Holmes, you look a bit upset. Did you uncover something you didn't like?"

"Okay, people this is what we have deduced: Mrs. Grey was in the downstairs bedroom, and she had the rope. Moriarty had the knife in the kitchen. This leaves Frank Brown."

Holmes turned toward Frank who in turn tried to run out of the sitting room only to be stopped by an officer.

"Frank, you were the one with the gun. You killed Richard in the lounge, and then you carried him out to the garden. You wear the same-sized clothes as Richard, so you went upstairs and changed your clothes to hide the bloodstains. So, in conclusion, Frank killed Richard in the lounge with the gun."

As much as it pained him, Holmes turned to Moriarty.

"Moriarty you are free to go as well as Mrs. Grey. Thank you all for your patience."

Answer: The Gaslighting Murder

We all walked back down the stairs and outside. Mr. Dutton was still sitting on the porch where we had left him.

"Well, was I right? Are they all dead?"

"Unfortunately, yes, Mr. Dutton, they are all dead," I replied.

He placed his head in his hands. He didn't necessarily cry but just looked lost and forlorn.

"Mr. Dutton, could you tell us where you were at last night?"

"Where I was last night?"

"Yes, where were you last night?"

"I was at a friend's house."

"What friend would that be, Mr. Dutton?"

"Mr. Holmes, I don't see how this is relevant to the case."

"If you will answer my question, I will tell you the relevance."

"I was at a party at Professor Moriarty's house."

"A party, did the Professor not invite your wife? That seems awfully rude, don't you think?"

"It was an evening out for the guys."

"I see. You have a new gas stove, don't you?"

"Yes."

"Do you know how to light the pilot light on the stove?"

"Yes."

"So, that means you know what would happen if you blew out the pilot light."

Mr. Dutton sat there frowning. "He said no one would be able to tell what happened. He said it would look like they died in their sleep."

"He was right they did die in their sleep. The gas filled the house and suffocated them. Only the murderer would have known to relight the pilot light when they came home so they wouldn't suffer the same fate. You also checked each one, rolled them onto their sides to make it look more natural and made sure they were covered up to their necks. Clever Mr. Dutton but not perfect. Professor Moriarty will lead you wrong every time. Call for Scotland Yard, Watson."

Answer: The Beach Murder

"Excuse me. Why do you want me to arrest this man?"

"Simple sir, his story is preposterous. I was on that beach today when the storm hit. It was so dark that you couldn't see more than two meters in front of you. There wasn't any way you could have seen anyone running away from your wife or your wife at the bottom of the cliff for that matter."

"Are you calling me a liar?"

"No sir, but you don't know anything about the weather. Lightning travels faster that thunder so you would have seen the lightning and then heard the thunder instead of the other way around."

Answer: The Exter Murder

We went over the notes I had taken carefully and made our way to the sitting room.

"Well, it looks like we know who the killer is. Do any of you have anything else you would like to add to your previous statement before we reveal the killer?"

Everyone sat as still as a stone statue. I suppose they were hoping that if they didn't move, we would forget they were there. That didn't work.

"Very well, Watson, go bring the constable in so they are ready to arrest the killer."

I left the office and went to find the constable. He was standing in the porch smoking. I passed on Holmes' request, and he followed me back inside.

"Constable, would you please arrest Yvonne?"

Yvonne stood up immediately.

"I didn't kill Sir Exter."

"Yes, you did, and I can prove it... Let's see Yvonne has been seen many times sprinkling a suspicious spice into Sir Exter's food. She is always worried about where Edward is. Why would she be worried about where he is if she wasn't trying to hide something? Yvonne also knew that Allen had managed to steal Sir Exter's ruby, and she wanted it for herself. Edward saw her steal the ruby from Allen and sprinkling the spice into Sir Exter's food. Edward wasn't ever doing anything wrong since walking around the garden was part of his job."

Answer: The Double Train Murder

"How in the world do you know that they were shot at two different times?"

"Elementary, my dear Watson, the train was going 150 kilometers per hour so the sound of a gunshot from the front of the train would have reached the officer's ears faster than a gun being shot from the rear of the train. Therefore, the conductor was the first one to be shot."

Answer: The Suicide Scheme

By the time Scotland Yard got there, we had found other clues. The constable walked in, and I am still standing there with the woman's weight on my shoulder.

"Why are you standing there like that?"

"Call me crazy, but I just couldn't let her hang there swinging back and forth."

"Understandable. Let's get her down."

Holmes stood on the chair and cut the rope. We gently laid her down on the floor.

"Constable, the woman was murdered. She didn't commit suicide."

"What gave you that idea?"

"The chair that was under her feet was too short for her feet to reach. It was put there as an afterthought. Plus, I found this lying on the table."

Holmes handed the constable a note. One, the note was a simple letter "M."

"You know who leaves these notes at scenes, don't you?"

"Yes, the infamous Moriarty."

"Now you know who to look for."

Answer: The Candy Murders

"You said Moriarty killed all these men, but he had help."

"Yes, Watson. I just need to go to Scotland Yard and do some investigating."

"Let's go."

We arrived at Scotland Yard, and Holmes asked to speak to the Detective in charge of the case. Detective Grant came out of an office at the end of the hall.

"Hello, my name is Sherlock Holmes. I would like to help you solve these candy murders."

"I would appreciate all the help I can get. All my files are in my office. Right this way, gentlemen."

We walked into Detective Grant's office. His desk was littered with papers, files, and all sorts of stuff.

"Pardon the mess."

"Mess is a good way to solve things."

Grant laughed quickly. "I'll take that as a compliment, Mr. Holmes."

"Let's get at those files."

Grant would hand Holmes a file after he looked through it. Holmes would peruse it quickly and put it in a pile beside him. This went on for about an hour.

"I know who helped Moriarty kill all those men."

"Moriarty? You didn't say anything about Moriarty before."

"Sorry, it slipped my mind. Moriarty provided the men with candy, but someone provided Moriarty with the men. Each person went before the same judge George Standoff. This judge thought these men deserved a chance to decide their own fate. When a case came before him and he thought they were a good candidate for his "program," he would dismiss their case. He would then tell Moriarty where these men lived. Moriarty would show up with a box of candy and ask them if they were willing to gamble for their life. Moriarty would offer them a specific number of candies. One of these pieces was laced with cyanide. If the man chose a candy that had been poisoned, he would die. If he chose one that wasn't poisoned, then he survived. He was basically playing a game of chance with these men's lives, many of whom lost their lives because of this judge."

Answer: The Church Murder

"You know who killed Abigail just from me reading you the suspects and why they disliked Abigail?"

"Yes, think about it, Watson. Lord Westerly couldn't have killed her because he is blind. He could not see that far away to make an accurate shot. The Reverend couldn't have done it because he was in the middle of services at the time of the murder. That only leaves Margaret. She wanted her aunt's money. She figured once her aunt was dead, all her money would come to Margaret as she was the only living relative."

"Too bad for her she won't be able to spend it."

"If I know Abigail, she has left it to someone else in her will."

Answer: The Baker's Murder

"Watson, are you sure about this?"

"I'm as sure as you would be if you were looking at the clues. First off, Wilhelm didn't write this note. He didn't speak English well enough to have written this note. This note was written by the killer, and there is only one killer who signs his name with a letter "M." You need to find Professor Moriarty."

Conclusion

Thank you for making it through to the end of *Sherlock Puzzle Book (Volume 2)*. Let's hope it was entertaining and fun for you. I hope that you have enjoyed every single puzzle. You can enjoy them again by asking them to your family and friends to see if they, too, are as smart as Sherlock Holmes.

Finally, if you found this book useful in any way, a review on Amazon is always appreciated!

Connect with us on our Facebook page www.facebook.com/bluesourceandfriends and stay tuned to our latest book promotions and free giveaways.

Don't forget to check out the other Sherlock books:

Sherlock Puzzle Book (Volume 3): Spending A Day In London With Mycroft Holmes

Sherlock Puzzle Book (Volume 1-3): Compilation Of 3 Books With Additional Bonus Contents By Mrs. Hudson

Made in the USA
Middletown, DE
17 August 2019